This book belongs to:

Introduction

Welcome to your Betta Fish Log Book. This log book can be used if you have one or more than one Betta Fish in your home. Whether you're a novice or experienced, you'll find this log book very useful.

It is important to note however, that this book assumes the reader has other sources of information for Betta Fish pet care. The purpose of this book is to help you track your Betta Fish feeding times and tank maintenance. You can list your favorite pet care resources on the page provided.

Here are some tips to help you keep track of your pet Betta Fish feeding and maintenance needs:

*On **page 7** you can plan out both the feeding schedule and tank maintenance schedule for your Betta Fish. (Use a pencil in case you need to make changes.)

*On **page 8** is a place for you to write down important books and websites for learning about pet care for your Betta Fish species. You can write the authors and titles of books/eBooks as well as some website names and internet links.

*The Maintenance Log pages are located before the Feeding Log pages. Write down the date on whichever days the water is either cycled or fully changed. On the Water Cycled column, write down the percentage (%) of the water cycled from the tank. You may write down the time for either the Water Cycled or Full Water Change to track the time of day it is done.

*The Maintenance Log pages also provide space for extra notes (such as water pH levels) and reminders for the future.

Continued next page…

Introduction (continued)

*The <u>Feeding Log</u> pages have 7-14 days worth of feeding times *per page* depending on how often you feed your Bettas. Use the check boxes if you've fed your fish close to their feeding time. The "Time Fed" column is good for if the feeding is later than usual.

*If you fast your fish once a week, write "Fast" in the Feeding Time for that day and leave the rest of the row blank.

*Below the Feeding Log pages is some space to write down notes. You can write about any changes you made, any reminders or plans about your Betta or Bettas' feeding, or other notes.

*Use bookmarks or sticky notes to mark your current places in the Maintenance Log and Feeding Log Sections. This way, you can quickly find where you left off.

*There are extra pages in this log book that have lines. Use these bonus pages to write about what you learn during caring for your beloved Betta Fish. You can also journal about your Betta, such as its behavior, its mood and what you find adorable about your fish.

May this log book help you in your Betta Fish journeys.

Betta Fish Name(s):

Nickname(s):

First day home:

Betta Fish species:

Fin type:

Tail type:

Colors:

Iridescence, Viridescence and Opaqueness:

Temperament:

Foods or favorite food

Type of Tank(s):

Description of inside the tank(s):

Betta Fish Name(s): _____

Nickname(s): _____

First day home: _____

Betta Fish species: _____

Fin type: _____

Tail type: _____

Colors: _____

Iridescence, Viridescence and Opaqueness: _____

Temperament: _____

Foods or favorite food _____

Type of Tank(s): _____

Description of inside the tank(s):

_____

_____

_____

My Betta's Regular Home Cleaning/Maintenance Schedule:

(<u>Use a pencil</u> to write on this page so you can make changes later)

SUN	MON	TUES	WED	THUR	FRI	SAT

My Betta's Regular Feeding Schedule:

SUN	MON	TUES	WED	THUR	FRI	SAT

My Favorite Resources for Betta Fish Care

Books and eBooks on Betta Fish Pet Care:

AUTHOR	BOOK OR eBOOK

Websites and Online Resources for Betta Fish Pet Care:

NAME/TITLE	WEBSITE LINK OR HOMEPAGE

My Favorite Resources for Betta Fish Care

Books and eBooks on Betta Fish Pet Care:

AUTHOR	BOOK OR eBOOK

Websites and Online Resources for Betta Fish Pet Care:

NAME/TITLE	WEBSITE LINK OR HOMEPAGE

BETTA TANK MAINTENANCE LOG SECTION

Maintenance Log for My Betta(s) Home

Date	Water Cycled	Full Water Change	Tank Cleaning Notes

OTHER NOTES:

Maintenance Log for My Betta(s) Home

Date	Water Cycled	Full Water Change	*Tank Cleaning Notes*

OTHER NOTES:

Maintenance Log for My Betta(s) Home

Date	Water Cycled	Full Water Change	Tank Cleaning Notes

OTHER NOTES:

Maintenance Log for My Betta(s) Home

Date	Water Cycled	Full Water Change	*Tank Cleaning Notes*

OTHER NOTES:

Maintenance Log for My Betta(s) Home

Date	Water Cycled	Full Water Change	Tank Cleaning Notes

OTHER NOTES:

Maintenance Log for My Betta(s) Home

Date	Water Cycled	Full Water Change	Tank Cleaning Notes

OTHER NOTES:

Maintenance Log for My Betta(s) Home

Date	Water Cycled	Full Water Change	*Tank Cleaning Notes*

OTHER NOTES:

Maintenance Log for My Betta(s) Home

Date	Water Cycled	Full Water Change	*Tank Cleaning Notes*

OTHER NOTES:

Maintenance Log for My Betta(s) Home

Date	Water Cycled	Full Water Change	*Tank Cleaning Notes*

OTHER NOTES:

Maintenance Log for My Betta(s) Home

Date	Water Cycled	Full Water Change	Tank Cleaning Notes

OTHER NOTES:

Maintenance Log for My Betta(s) Home

Date	Water Cycled	Full Water Change	Tank Cleaning Notes

OTHER NOTES:

Maintenance Log for My Betta(s) Home

Date	Water Cycled	Full Water Change	*Tank Cleaning Notes*

OTHER NOTES:

Maintenance Log for My Betta(s) Home

Date	Water Cycled	Full Water Change	Tank Cleaning Notes

OTHER NOTES:

Maintenance Log for My Betta(s) Home

Date	Water Cycled	Full Water Change	*Tank Cleaning Notes*

OTHER NOTES:

Maintenance Log for My Betta(s) Home

Date	Water Cycled	Full Water Change	*Tank Cleaning Notes*

OTHER NOTES:

Maintenance Log for My Betta(s) Home

Date	Water Cycled	Full Water Change	*Tank Cleaning Notes*

OTHER NOTES:

Maintenance Log for My Betta(s) Home

Date	Water Cycled	Full Water Change	Tank Cleaning Notes

OTHER NOTES:

Maintenance Log for My Betta(s) Home

Date	Water Cycled	Full Water Change	*Tank Cleaning Notes*

OTHER NOTES:

Maintenance Log for My Betta(s) Home

Date	Water Cycled	Full Water Change	*Tank Cleaning Notes*

OTHER NOTES:

Maintenance Log for My Betta(s) Home

Date	Water Cycled	Full Water Change	Tank Cleaning Notes

OTHER NOTES:

BETTA
FEEDING LOG
SECTION

Feeding Log for My Betta(s)

Date	Feeding Time	Time Fed	Food Type & Amount
	☐		
	☐		
	☐		
	☐		
	☐		
	☐		
	☐		
	☐		
	☐		
	☐		
	☐		
	☐		
	☐		
	☐		

NOTES:

Feeding Log for My Betta(s)

Date	Feeding Time	Time Fed	Food Type & Amount
	☐		
	☐		
	☐		
	☐		
	☐		
	☐		
	☐		
	☐		
	☐		
	☐		
	☐		
	☐		
	☐		
	☐		

NOTES:

Feeding Log for My Betta(s)

Date	Feeding Time	Time Fed	Food Type & Amount
	☐		
	☐		
	☐		
	☐		
	☐		
	☐		
	☐		
	☐		
	☐		
	☐		
	☐		
	☐		
	☐		
	☐		

NOTES:

Feeding Log for My Betta(s)

Date	Feeding Time	Time Fed	Food Type & Amount
	☐		
	☐		
	☐		
	☐		
	☐		
	☐		
	☐		
	☐		
	☐		
	☐		
	☐		
	☐		
	☐		
	☐		

NOTES:

Feeding Log for My Betta(s)

Date	Feeding Time	Time Fed	Food Type & Amount
	☐		
	☐		
	☐		
	☐		
	☐		
	☐		
	☐		
	☐		
	☐		
	☐		
	☐		
	☐		
	☐		
	☐		

NOTES:

Feeding Log for My Betta(s)

Date	Feeding Time	Time Fed	Food Type & Amount
		☐	
		☐	
		☐	
		☐	
		☐	
		☐	
		☐	
		☐	
		☐	
		☐	
		☐	
		☐	
		☐	
		☐	

NOTES:

Feeding Log for My Betta(s)

Date	Feeding Time	Time Fed	Food Type & Amount
	☐		
	☐		
	☐		
	☐		
	☐		
	☐		
	☐		
	☐		
	☐		
	☐		
	☐		
	☐		
	☐		
	☐		

NOTES:

Feeding Log for My Betta(s)

Date	Feeding Time	Time Fed	Food Type & Amount
	☐		
	☐		
	☐		
	☐		
	☐		
	☐		
	☐		
	☐		
	☐		
	☐		
	☐		
	☐		
	☐		
	☐		

NOTES:

Feeding Log for My Betta(s)

Date	Feeding Time	Time Fed	Food Type & Amount
	☐		
	☐		
	☐		
	☐		
	☐		
	☐		
	☐		
	☐		
	☐		
	☐		
	☐		
	☐		
	☐		
	☐		

NOTES:

Feeding Log for My Betta(s)

Date	Feeding Time	Time Fed	Food Type & Amount
	☐		
	☐		
	☐		
	☐		
	☐		
	☐		
	☐		
	☐		
	☐		
	☐		
	☐		
	☐		
	☐		
	☐		

NOTES:

Feeding Log for My Betta(s)

Date	Feeding Time	Time Fed	Food Type & Amount
	☐		
	☐		
	☐		
	☐		
	☐		
	☐		
	☐		
	☐		
	☐		
	☐		
	☐		
	☐		
	☐		
	☐		

NOTES:

Feeding Log for My Betta(s)

Date	Feeding Time	Time Fed	Food Type & Amount
	☐		
	☐		
	☐		
	☐		
	☐		
	☐		
	☐		
	☐		
	☐		
	☐		
	☐		
	☐		
	☐		
	☐		

NOTES:

Feeding Log for My Betta(s)

Date	Feeding Time	Time Fed	Food Type & Amount
	☐		
	☐		
	☐		
	☐		
	☐		
	☐		
	☐		
	☐		
	☐		
	☐		
	☐		
	☐		
	☐		
	☐		

NOTES:

Feeding Log for My Betta(s)

Date	Feeding Time	Time Fed	Food Type & Amount
	☐		
	☐		
	☐		
	☐		
	☐		
	☐		
	☐		
	☐		
	☐		
	☐		
	☐		
	☐		
	☐		
	☐		

NOTES:

Feeding Log for My Betta(s)

Date	Feeding Time	Time Fed	Food Type & Amount
	☐		
	☐		
	☐		
	☐		
	☐		
	☐		
	☐		
	☐		
	☐		
	☐		
	☐		
	☐		
	☐		
	☐		

NOTES:

Feeding Log for My Betta(s)

Date	Feeding Time	Time Fed	Food Type & Amount
	☐		
	☐		
	☐		
	☐		
	☐		
	☐		
	☐		
	☐		
	☐		
	☐		
	☐		
	☐		
	☐		
	☐		

NOTES:

Feeding Log for My Betta(s)

Date	Feeding Time	Time Fed	Food Type & Amount
	☐		
	☐		
	☐		
	☐		
	☐		
	☐		
	☐		
	☐		
	☐		
	☐		
	☐		
	☐		
	☐		
	☐		

NOTES:

Feeding Log for My Betta(s)

Date	Feeding Time	Time Fed	Food Type & Amount
	☐		
	☐		
	☐		
	☐		
	☐		
	☐		
	☐		
	☐		
	☐		
	☐		
	☐		
	☐		
	☐		
	☐		

NOTES:

Feeding Log for My Betta(s)

Date	Feeding Time	Time Fed	Food Type & Amount
	☐		
	☐		
	☐		
	☐		
	☐		
	☐		
	☐		
	☐		
	☐		
	☐		
	☐		
	☐		
	☐		
	☐		

NOTES:

Feeding Log for My Betta(s)

Date	Feeding Time	Time Fed	Food Type & Amount
	☐		
	☐		
	☐		
	☐		
	☐		
	☐		
	☐		
	☐		
	☐		
	☐		
	☐		
	☐		
	☐		

NOTES:

Feeding Log for My Betta(s)

Date	Feeding Time	Time Fed	Food Type & Amount
		☐	
		☐	
		☐	
		☐	
		☐	
		☐	
		☐	
		☐	
		☐	
		☐	
		☐	
		☐	
		☐	
		☐	

NOTES:

Feeding Log for My Betta(s)

Date	Feeding Time	Time Fed	Food Type & Amount
	☐		
	☐		
	☐		
	☐		
	☐		
	☐		
	☐		
	☐		
	☐		
	☐		
	☐		
	☐		
	☐		
	☐		

NOTES:

Feeding Log for My Betta(s)

Date	Feeding Time	Time Fed	Food Type & Amount
	☐		
	☐		
	☐		
	☐		
	☐		
	☐		
	☐		
	☐		
	☐		
	☐		
	☐		
	☐		
	☐		
	☐		

NOTES:

Feeding Log for My Betta(s)

Date	Feeding Time	Time Fed	Food Type & Amount
	☐		
	☐		
	☐		
	☐		
	☐		
	☐		
	☐		
	☐		
	☐		
	☐		
	☐		
	☐		
	☐		
	☐		

NOTES:

Feeding Log for My Betta(s)

Date	Feeding Time	Time Fed	Food Type & Amount
	☐		
	☐		
	☐		
	☐		
	☐		
	☐		
	☐		
	☐		
	☐		
	☐		
	☐		
	☐		
	☐		
	☐		

NOTES:

Feeding Log for My Betta(s)

Date	Feeding Time	Time Fed	Food Type & Amount
	☐		
	☐		
	☐		
	☐		
	☐		
	☐		
	☐		
	☐		
	☐		
	☐		
	☐		
	☐		
	☐		
	☐		

NOTES:

Feeding Log for My Betta(s)

Date	Feeding Time	Time Fed	Food Type & Amount
	☐		
	☐		
	☐		
	☐		
	☐		
	☐		
	☐		
	☐		
	☐		
	☐		
	☐		
	☐		
	☐		
	☐		

NOTES:

Feeding Log for My Betta(s)

Date	Feeding Time	Time Fed	Food Type & Amount
	☐		
	☐		
	☐		
	☐		
	☐		
	☐		
	☐		
	☐		
	☐		
	☐		
	☐		
	☐		
	☐		
	☐		

NOTES:

Feeding Log for My Betta(s)

Date	Feeding Time	Time Fed	Food Type & Amount
	☐		
	☐		
	☐		
	☐		
	☐		
	☐		
	☐		
	☐		
	☐		
	☐		
	☐		
	☐		
	☐		
	☐		

NOTES:

Feeding Log for My Betta(s)

Date	Feeding Time	Time Fed	Food Type & Amount
	☐		
	☐		
	☐		
	☐		
	☐		
	☐		
	☐		
	☐		
	☐		
	☐		
	☐		
	☐		
	☐		
	☐		

NOTES:

Feeding Log for My Betta(s)

Date	Feeding Time	Time Fed	Food Type & Amount
	☐		
	☐		
	☐		
	☐		
	☐		
	☐		
	☐		
	☐		
	☐		
	☐		
	☐		
	☐		
	☐		
	☐		

NOTES:

Feeding Log for My Betta(s)

Date	Feeding Time	Time Fed	Food Type & Amount
	☐		
	☐		
	☐		
	☐		
	☐		
	☐		
	☐		
	☐		
	☐		
	☐		
	☐		
	☐		
	☐		
	☐		

NOTES:

Feeding Log for My Betta(s)

Date	Feeding Time	Time Fed	Food Type & Amount
	☐		
	☐		
	☐		
	☐		
	☐		
	☐		
	☐		
	☐		
	☐		
	☐		
	☐		
	☐		
	☐		
	☐		

NOTES:

Feeding Log for My Betta(s)

Date	Feeding Time	Time Fed	Food Type & Amount
	☐		
	☐		
	☐		
	☐		
	☐		
	☐		
	☐		
	☐		
	☐		
	☐		
	☐		
	☐		
	☐		
	☐		

NOTES:

Feeding Log for My Betta(s)

Date	Feeding Time	Time Fed	Food Type & Amount
	☐		
	☐		
	☐		
	☐		
	☐		
	☐		
	☐		
	☐		
	☐		
	☐		
	☐		
	☐		
	☐		
	☐		

NOTES:

Feeding Log for My Betta(s)

Date	Feeding Time	Time Fed	Food Type & Amount
	☐		
	☐		
	☐		
	☐		
	☐		
	☐		
	☐		
	☐		
	☐		
	☐		
	☐		
	☐		
	☐		
	☐		

NOTES:

Feeding Log for My Betta(s)

Date	Feeding Time	Time Fed	Food Type & Amount
	☐		
	☐		
	☐		
	☐		
	☐		
	☐		
	☐		
	☐		
	☐		
	☐		
	☐		
	☐		
	☐		
	☐		

NOTES:

Feeding Log for My Betta(s)

Date	Feeding Time	Time Fed	Food Type & Amount
	☐		
	☐		
	☐		
	☐		
	☐		
	☐		
	☐		
	☐		
	☐		
	☐		
	☐		
	☐		
	☐		
	☐		

NOTES:

Feeding Log for My Betta(s)

Date	Feeding Time	Time Fed	Food Type & Amount
	☐		
	☐		
	☐		
	☐		
	☐		
	☐		
	☐		
	☐		
	☐		
	☐		
	☐		
	☐		
	☐		
	☐		

NOTES:

Feeding Log for My Betta(s)

Date	Feeding Time	Time Fed	Food Type & Amount
		☐	
		☐	
		☐	
		☐	
		☐	
		☐	
		☐	
		☐	
		☐	
		☐	
		☐	
		☐	
		☐	
		☐	

NOTES:

Feeding Log for My Betta(s)

Date	Feeding Time	Time Fed	Food Type & Amount
	☐		
	☐		
	☐		
	☐		
	☐		
	☐		
	☐		
	☐		
	☐		
	☐		
	☐		
	☐		
	☐		
	☐		

NOTES:

Feeding Log for My Betta(s)

Date	Feeding Time	Time Fed	Food Type & Amount
	☐		
	☐		
	☐		
	☐		
	☐		
	☐		
	☐		
	☐		
	☐		
	☐		
	☐		
	☐		
	☐		
	☐		

NOTES:

Feeding Log for My Betta(s)

Date	Feeding Time	Time Fed	Food Type & Amount
	☐		
	☐		
	☐		
	☐		
	☐		
	☐		
	☐		
	☐		
	☐		
	☐		
	☐		
	☐		
	☐		
	☐		

NOTES:

Feeding Log for My Betta(s)

Date	Feeding Time	Time Fed	Food Type & Amount
	☐		
	☐		
	☐		
	☐		
	☐		
	☐		
	☐		
	☐		
	☐		
	☐		
	☐		
	☐		
	☐		
	☐		

NOTES:

Feeding Log for My Betta(s)

Date	Feeding Time	Time Fed	Food Type & Amount
	☐		
	☐		
	☐		
	☐		
	☐		
	☐		
	☐		
	☐		
	☐		
	☐		
	☐		
	☐		
	☐		
	☐		

NOTES:

Feeding Log for My Betta(s)

Date	Feeding Time	Time Fed	Food Type & Amount
	☐		
	☐		
	☐		
	☐		
	☐		
	☐		
	☐		
	☐		
	☐		
	☐		
	☐		
	☐		
	☐		
	☐		

NOTES:

Feeding Log for My Betta(s)

Date	Feeding Time	Time Fed	Food Type & Amount
	☐		
	☐		
	☐		
	☐		
	☐		
	☐		
	☐		
	☐		
	☐		
	☐		
	☐		
	☐		
	☐		
	☐		

NOTES:

Feeding Log for My Betta(s)

Date	Feeding Time	Time Fed	Food Type & Amount
	☐		
	☐		
	☐		
	☐		
	☐		
	☐		
	☐		
	☐		
	☐		
	☐		
	☐		
	☐		
	☐		
	☐		

NOTES:

Feeding Log for My Betta(s)

Date	Feeding Time	Time Fed	Food Type & Amount
	☐		
	☐		
	☐		
	☐		
	☐		
	☐		
	☐		
	☐		
	☐		
	☐		
	☐		
	☐		
	☐		
	☐		

NOTES:

Feeding Log for My Betta(s)

Date	Feeding Time	Time Fed	Food Type & Amount
	☐		
	☐		
	☐		
	☐		
	☐		
	☐		
	☐		
	☐		
	☐		
	☐		
	☐		
	☐		
	☐		
	☐		

NOTES:

Feeding Log for My Betta(s)

Date	Feeding Time	Time Fed	Food Type & Amount
	☐		
	☐		
	☐		
	☐		
	☐		
	☐		
	☐		
	☐		
	☐		
	☐		
	☐		
	☐		
	☐		

NOTES:

Feeding Log for My Betta(s)

Date	Feeding Time	Time Fed	Food Type & Amount
	☐		
	☐		
	☐		
	☐		
	☐		
	☐		
	☐		
	☐		
	☐		
	☐		
	☐		
	☐		
	☐		
	☐		

NOTES:

Feeding Log for My Betta(s)

Date	Feeding Time	Time Fed	Food Type & Amount
	☐		
	☐		
	☐		
	☐		
	☐		
	☐		
	☐		
	☐		
	☐		
	☐		
	☐		
	☐		
	☐		
	☐		

NOTES:

Feeding Log for My Betta(s)

Date	Feeding Time	Time Fed	Food Type & Amount
	☐		
	☐		
	☐		
	☐		
	☐		
	☐		
	☐		
	☐		
	☐		
	☐		
	☐		
	☐		
	☐		
	☐		

NOTES:

Feeding Log for My Betta(s)

Date	Feeding Time	Time Fed	Food Type & Amount
	☐		
	☐		
	☐		
	☐		
	☐		
	☐		
	☐		
	☐		
	☐		
	☐		
	☐		
	☐		
	☐		
	☐		

NOTES:

You have a few more pages of Feeding Logs left.
Time to get another log book!

You can find this log book and more log books
and journals by Sara A. Watts at
https://www.amazon.com/author/sara-a-watts

Feeding Log for My Betta(s)

Date	Feeding Time	Time Fed	Food Type & Amount
	☐		
	☐		
	☐		
	☐		
	☐		
	☐		
	☐		
	☐		
	☐		
	☐		
	☐		
	☐		
	☐		
	☐		

NOTES:

Feeding Log for My Betta(s)

Date	Feeding Time	Time Fed	Food Type & Amount
	☐		
	☐		
	☐		
	☐		
	☐		
	☐		
	☐		
	☐		
	☐		
	☐		
	☐		
	☐		
	☐		
	☐		

NOTES:

Feeding Log for My Betta(s)

Date	Feeding Time	Time Fed	Food Type & Amount
	☐		
	☐		
	☐		
	☐		
	☐		
	☐		
	☐		
	☐		
	☐		
	☐		
	☐		
	☐		
	☐		
	☐		

NOTES:

Feeding Log for My Betta(s)

Date	Feeding Time	Time Fed	Food Type & Amount
	☐		
	☐		
	☐		
	☐		
	☐		
	☐		
	☐		
	☐		
	☐		
	☐		
	☐		
	☐		
	☐		
	☐		

NOTES:

Feeding Log for My Betta(s)

Date	Feeding Time	Time Fed	Food Type & Amount
		☐	
		☐	
		☐	
		☐	
		☐	
		☐	
		☐	
		☐	
		☐	
		☐	
		☐	
		☐	
		☐	
		☐	

NOTES:

BETTA
JOURNAL AND NOTES
SECTION

You're nearly done...
time to get another log book!

You can find this log book and more log books
and journals by Sara A. Watts at
https://www.amazon.com/author/sara-a-watts

Made in the USA
Lexington, KY
01 June 2019